YOUR GOD, MY GOD

A Woman's Workshop on Ruth

Student's Manual

Anne Wilcox

Books in this series—

YOUR GOD, MY GOD

A Woman's Workshop on Ruth

Student's Manual

Anne Wilcox

Lamplighter Books Grand Rapids, Michigan
Zondervan Publishing House

Your God, My God
Copyright © 1985 by The Zondervan Corporation
Grand Rapids, Michigan

ISBN 0-310-44711-9

Edited by Kin Millen and Janet Kobobel

Printed in the United States of America

88   89   90   91   92   93   94 / CH / 12   11   10   9   8   7   6   5   4   3

To
Coralie Wilcox
my mother-in-law
and dear friend

CONTENTS

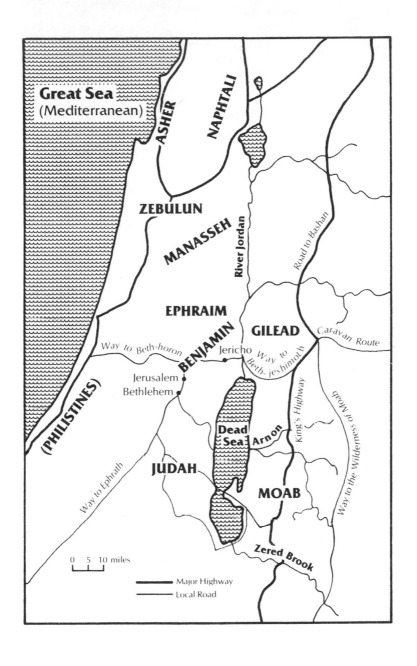

Great Sea
(Mediterranean)

ASHER

NAPHTALI

ZEBULUN

MANASSEH

River Jordan

Road to Bashan

EPHRAIM

GILEAD

Caravan Route

BENJAMIN

Way to Beth-horon

Jericho

Way to Beth-jeshimoth

Jerusalem

Bethlehem

(PHILISTINES)

King's Highway

Dead Sea

Arnon

Way to the Wilderness of Moab

JUDAH

MOAB

Way to Ephrath

Zered Brook

0   5   10 miles

———— Major Highway
———— Local Road

PREFACE

You can use this Bible study manual to increase your comprehension of the Book of Ruth, and to facilitate personal interaction with its message. The lessons are designed for home Bible studies, small discussion groups, or personal study. Each lesson contains questions, charts, and projects designed for creative observations, careful interpretations, and contemporary applications. Study skills transferable to other narrative portions of the Bible are taught through this workshop, but its primary focus is to impart skills for living faithfully in a faithless age.

Since Ruth comprises an ancient Jewish story, the first four chapters of this study are written to help our contemporary minds explore the cultural and historical influences Ruth experienced three thousand years ago. She gleaned wheat by hand. Today we gather it in stereo-equipped combines. Despite the technological differences of our eras, Ruth faced the same moral and spiritual decisions that confront us today.

In this study, you will also become acquainted with Boaz, whose obedience surpasses the letter of the law and expresses the true spirit of God's commands. As you watch Naomi, you will see the struggles and choices of a woman passing through seasons of heartache and seasons of blessing. As each character is brought into sharper focus through your study, you will see the hope they give us for living godly lives in the midst of a godless age.

Throughout the Book of Ruth, you will observe a God who is intimately at work in the lives of all who respond to Him by faith. You will see that though He allows loss and heartache to touch His people, He has not lost control.

The final verses of Ruth testify to His sovereign control of the world's history. To Israel these verses spoke of the national hope that came through King David's leadership. To us the verses speak of the Davidic line through which the world's Savior has come.

May you embrace God wholeheartedly as Ruth did, and may the next generation observe and say, "Your God Shall Be My God!"

ACKNOWLEDGMENTS

My first in-depth study of the Book of Ruth began while team-teaching a Bible study with D.D. Mitchell. I thank her for critiquing the manuscript and praying it to completion. Her mastery of both the Scriptures and the English language have made an invaluable contribution to this study.

I am deeply grateful for the enthusiastic support of Dr. Ronald B. Allen. His research suggestions and teaching materials have added new dimensions to my understanding of this Hebrew story.

Without Kin Millen, A Woman's Workshop on Ruth would still be in the raw. In the middle of the project he graciously provided professional advice and assistance. Through the final rigors of editing his encouragement and wit made the process not only tolerable but also completely enjoyable.

Many times in the final stages of a book the end seems impossible to achieve. At one of those moments, Jennifer

Batts offered to help with the typing. Without her ministry, the deadline would still be unmet.

My deepest thanks goes to my supportive family. My husband graciously accepted my marriage to the typewriter during many hours of research and writing. My parents, Dick and Dorothy Hagerman, generously provided opportunities to continue my education in writing and my parents-in-law, Cliff and Coralie Wilcox, volunteered hours of grandparenting for two-year-old Jaime as I worked to meet deadlines.

1

DOING YOUR OWN THING IN ANTIQUITY

Imagine for a moment that you and I are seated in a theater. We are chatting together and poring over programs as we anticipate the performance of *Romeo and Juliet.* Suddenly the house lights dim, the room darkens, and all eyes focus on the veiled stage. As the curtains part, the expectant silence of the audience disintegrates into fidgeting and whispering. You and I look at each other in amazement. The stage holds condominiums instead of castles, and the actors wear three-piece suits instead of sixteenth-century dress.

Before we criticize the backdrop crew, let's consider the problem of approaching biblical narratives without thinking about the historical setting. Many times we drag along our twentieth-century perspectives and create something as ridiculous as Romeo scaling the balcony of a condominium.

In the next few questions, we will leave our modern era

behind and paint an appropriate backdrop for the study of Ruth.

1. The major periods of Israel's history can be illustrated in the following table. Read Ruth 1:1 and circle the historical period that provides the background for this narrative.

Major Periods of the Old Testament and New Testament

CREATION	PATRIARCHS	EXODUS	JUDGES	UNITED KINGDOM
Adam	Abraham, Isaac, Jacob, Joseph	Moses		Saul, David, Solomon

Divided Kingdom	Israel Judah	Exile	Restoration	400 Silent Years	Christ

2. The events of this period of history are recorded for us in the Book of Judges. Judges 2:16–19 summarizes this era's spiritual tenor. As you read the passage below: a) underline the people's actions and attitudes; b) circle God's actions and attitudes.

Then the Lord raised up judges, who saved them out of the hands of these raiders. Yet they would not listen to their judges but prostituted themselves to other gods and worshiped them. Unlike their fathers, they quickly turned from the way in which their fathers had walked, the way of obedience to the Lord's commands. Whenever the Lord raised up a judge for them, he was with the judge and saved them out of the hands of their enemies as long as the judge lived; for the Lord had compassion on them as they groaned under those who oppressed and afflicted them. But when the judge died, the people returned to ways even more corrupt than those of their fathers, following other gods and serving and worshiping them. They refused to give up their evil practices and stubborn ways.

Judges 2:16–19

3. What word or phrase would you use to describe the Israelites' hearts during the period of the judges? _____

_____

_____

4. List the attributes God expressed during these generations. _____

_____

_____

_____

5. Many years before the judges, warnings against spiritual forgetfulness were given by God through His spokesman Moses. Compare the instructions in Deuteronomy 6:1–9 with the appraisal of the first generation in the era of the judges (Judges 2:10). Who was to blame for this spiritual drought? _____

_____

_____

6. In your own words, rewrite the epitaph for this historical period found in Judges 21:25. _____

_____

_____

7. The entire Book of Ruth could easily fit on the daily newspaper's front page. Read the book in one sitting. When you finish, create an appropriate epitaph for Ruth's life. _____

_____

_____

8. What epitaph would you give your generation? _____

_____

_____

9. Analyze an opinion you have recently heard concerning a contemporary moral issue by answering the following questions:

a. What general philosophy of life does this opinion reflect? _____

_____

_____

b. What standards govern the life of the person holding this opinion? _____

_____

_____

10. Does one individual have any hope for influencing society today? Before answering this question, try the following project:

a. List current philosophies or situations that you feel contradict God's moral laws. _____

_____

_____

_____

_____

_____

_____

_____

_____

b. Look over the options below. Choose one action you can accomplish this week to influence change in one of the areas you listed.

1) Write my concerns in a letter to my government representative.

2) Register a complaint with my radio or T.V. station.

3) Write an editorial in my local newspaper.

4) Take an evening to teach my children God's view of this problem.

5) Make sure my own life models God's instructions about this issue.

6) Other:

*11. Look back at the epitaph you wrote for your generation. What do you wish the epitaph would say? Ask the Lord to use you in bringing about the change you desire for your generation and the ones to follow.

*Questions preceded by an asterisk throughout the book are for personal thought and reflection.

2

CROSS-CULTURAL ADJUSTMENTS

"Matt, how was France?"

This collegiate basketball player was a special friend of our family, and we had been eager to quiz him ever since his team had returned from Europe. The first story he shared was typical of cross-cultural surprises.

A lavish meal had been prepared for this American basketball team before one of the games in France. After he had devoured the delicious food, Matt was politely asked if he wanted more. Eager to answer in the national language, he pulled out an English-French dictionary and searched for the word "full." Finding it quickly, he eloquently replied in French, "No thank you, I'm full." His nonverbal communication included rubbing his stomach.

The response he received baffled him. Bursting into laughter, the server rushed to her colleagues and repeated his response. Matt watched in confusion as more people began enjoying the obvious hilarity of his answer. Finally an interpreter came to his aid and explained that he had used an idiom meaning, "No thank you, I'm pregnant."

In most cross-cultural experiences, the language barrier is one of the most difficult hurdles to cross. Fortunately for Ruth, her language shared grammatical similarities with Hebrew. This, no doubt, aided her in leaving her Moabite culture as she stepped into the world of the Israelites, first as the wife of an Israelite in a Moabite culture and finally as an alien in the nation of Israel.

Ruth's words of commitment to Naomi suggest she was ready to adopt a new culture (Ruth 1:16–18). She wanted to worship a new God, she was willing to adjust to new customs, and she was committed to remain in the new land for the rest of her life.

Some of the adjustment difficulties Ruth would encounter grew out of past foreign relations between Moab and Israel. Interaction between the two countries had been filled with political tensions and wars. The challenge facing Ruth was not her willingness to adapt cross-culturally, but the willingness of her new nation to accept her.

1. Underline all the times in the Book of Ruth that the author mentions Moab or Ruth's identification with this country. How many references did you discover? Why do you think the author gives us this repetition? _____

_____

_____

_____

2. Compare the origin of the Moabites (Genesis 19:27– 38) with the origin of the Israelites (Genesis 12:1–3). How do you suppose the Israelites felt about their distant cousins based on these beginnings? _____

_____

_____

_____

3. When Ruth married Mahlon, she was introduced to another religion. When she left Moab, she chose to adopt Naomi's God as her own. Investigate the religion Ruth was leaving. See if you can discover the names of her local gods and the activities involved in worshiping these Moabite deities. (Information can be obtained from a Bible encyclopedia under the heading "Moab" and under the specific names of each god.) _____

_____

_____

_____

_____

_____

_____

_____

_____

4. God gave Israel many foreign relations policies through His servant Moses. Deuteronomy 2:9 and 23:3–6 are instructions concerning the policies with Moab. Compare the instructions in Deuteronomy 23:3–6 with the words of Israel's elders found in Ruth 4:11–12.

Instructions from Deut. 23:3–6	Blessings from Ruth 4:11–12

Instructions from Deut. 23:3–6	Blessings from Ruth 4:11–12

5. How would you explain the contrast of the previous chart? _____

_____

_____

_____

6. Judges 3:12–30 records a national conflict between Moab and Israel during the period of the judges. Because of this episode, what barriers might Ruth have encountered when she first arrived in Bethlehem? _____

_____

_____

7. Numbers 25:1–3 records a religious conflict between Moab and Israel. How do you think the Israelite women initially reacted to a Moabite woman in their midst? _____

_____

_____

8. How would you explain the blessing and praise these women gave Ruth (Ruth 4:15)? _____

9. What cultures or groups of people struggle to find acceptance in your community? Why do you think the problem exists? _____

_____

_____

10. Are there certain cultural groups that you have difficulty relating to or accepting? Identify the reasons for your feelings. _____

_____

_____

_____

11. Are there people in your own home whom you find hard to accept? Evaluate why you have difficulty relating to them. Are their personalities and attitudes different than yours or too much like yours? Must they accomplish certain achievements to gain your acceptance? _____

_____

_____

_____

12. Analyze your feelings toward those in your church who have come to Christ out of a different background or at a different time than your experience. _____

_____

_____

_____

_____

13. In your opinion, what criteria must a person meet before being accepted by God? _____

_____

_____

14. What does God's treatment of Ruth show you about His standards for acceptance? _____

_____

_____

*15. Take time before God to compare your standards of acceptance of others with His standards. Prayerfully choose one person who came to mind as you worked on questions 9–12. List specific ways your criteria of acceptance can begin to resemble God's as you interact with this person. _____

_____

_____

_____

_____

_____

_____

3

SCENES FROM A LOVE STORY

The love story in the Book of Ruth varies greatly from those usually found on the top ten best-seller list. Every scene demonstrates the commitment and responsibility required of true love. The dialogues of this short story are filled with words of encouragement and support. The characters consistently choose what is right—not what is convenient. The author has truly painted a skillful portrait of godly living.

As if that were not enough, this author-craftsman shapes his work with literary excellence. All the elements of a skillful plot exist in this short narrative. The story begins with a tragedy and moves to obstacles that must be resolved. A hero is introduced who can save the heroine, and their relationship progresses to a climactic meeting that involves a marriage proposal. Another obstacle is introduced that holds the tension of the story until the end. Finally all problems are resolved, and the story ends with a happy marriage that provides prosperity and security for the rest of life.

Listed below are the elements that contribute to a well-designed plot (adapted from Leland Ryken's *The Literature of the Bible*). Read through the elements and their definitions. Identify the scenes from Ruth that represent each element.

Elements of a Skillful Plot	Representative Scenes from Ruth
1. *Exposition*—background material that brings the reader up to date with the character's present circumstances.	1.
2. *Inciting Force*—circumstances that get the story moving.	2.
3. *Rising Action*—interesting developments that progress the plot.	3.
4. *Turning Point*—an entrance in the story of a possible solution to the existing conflicts.	4.
5. *Complications*—the possible solution encounters obstacles at this point in the story.	5.
6. *Climax*—the point of highest dramatic tension in the narrative.	6.
7. *Denouement*—the final outcome of the story's complications.	7.

8. The Book of Ruth contains an abundance of personal interaction between its characters. More than fifty of the eighty-four verses are dialogue. Use a Bible you can mark in to color-code each character's words. Use red for underlining Naomi's words, blue for underlining Ruth's, and yellow for Boaz's.

9. When you have finished underlining, review the Book of Ruth, reading only Naomi's words. Judging from her words, how would you describe this woman's personality and appearance? _____

_____

_____

_____

10. Read the Book of Ruth again. This time read only Ruth's words. Describe the character qualities Ruth demonstrates as she speaks. _____

_____

_____

_____

11. During the third reading of Ruth, read only Boaz's words. How would you describe this man's personality and character? _____

_____

_____

_____

12. Reflect on your conversations this last week. How do your words compare with the encouraging and supportive conversations found in Ruth? _____

_____

_____

_____

*13. Consider Jesus' words, "For out of the overflow of the heart the mouth speaks" (Matthew 12:34). Prayerfully evaluate your heart's condition in relation to the words you have spoken recently.

14. Write the primary message of the Book of Ruth in your own words. Decide which scene illustrates this message. _____

_____

_____

_____

_____

_____

15. How can this message affect your present circumstances? _____

_____

_____

_____

4

THOSE WHO KNOW YOUR NAME WILL TRUST IN YOU

We spent hours poring over baby name books. Our first child through adoption was due in a few short weeks, and we had to decide what to call him or her. We tried several combinations, but when we would finally find two names that sounded good together, their meanings bore no relationship. At the same time, when we found names with special meanings, they sounded terrible together. Again and again we rearranged and analyzed names. Finally we settled on a name for a boy and a name for a girl that suited us. When the birth call came, we were ready. The baby became Jaime Lynne, our "beloved, refreshing" little girl.

In Hebrew culture a name represented more than a special meaning. Knowing the name of someone meant knowing the character, behavior, and essence of that person. Therefore, the naming of a Hebrew child was an event of great importance.

The name was sometimes a description of the parent's desires for the child. Other times it represented a prophetic expression of the child's personality. Children were also named to represent events at their birth. Throughout Scripture one can also find accounts of a person's name being changed. In these cases, the change was to signal a new career, a new season of life, a new relationship to God, or a new character quality.

An examination of the names in the Book of Ruth contributes significant insights into the narrative. In the first four verses of chapter one, all the main characters are named except Boaz. Just by giving these names, the author is providing important information about each person.

Below is a list of the names in the Book of Ruth. Write the meaning you discover from a Bible encyclopedia or a Bible dictionary beside each name.

Names from Ruth	Name Meanings
Elimelech	
Naomi	
Mara	
Mahlon	
Kilion	
Orpah	
Ruth	
Boaz	
Obed	
Jesse	
David	

Names from Ruth	Name Meanings

Bethlehem

Moab

1. How did Elimelech represent his name's meaning through his actions and decisions? _____

_____

_____

_____

2. What was Naomi expressing by asking the townspeople to change her name? _____

_____

_____

_____

3. What significance might the names of Naomi's children have had on the family's decision to flee from the famine in Bethlehem? _____

_____

_____

4. Compare the name meanings of Ruth and Orpah. How did these Moabite women express the characteristics implied by their names?_____

_____

_____

_____

5. Boaz's name means "strength" or "fleetness." Describe the kinds of strengths (emotional, physical, or spiritual) you see Boaz possessing. _____

_____

_____

_____

6. What is the name of the other kinsman-redeemer in our story? Yet what was his motive in relinquishing his rights and responsibilities to Boaz? _____

_____

_____

_____

The Names of God in Ruth

"In Jesus' name I pray, Amen." Many people end their prayers with this line without ever thinking about it. What does it mean to know God's name? In the Old Testament God revealed Himself to His people in many ways. One of those ways was the disclosure of names that reflected His character and essence. The volunteering of His names to His people expresses the desire that they know God. These names encompass both the transcendent holiness of God and His intimate involvement in everyday life.

The Book of Ruth uses two of God's names. They are listed below with their Hebrew designation, their representation in the New International Version, and their definitions.

Hebrew Designation	NIV Translation	Name Definition
YHWH or Yahweh	LORD	He who is truly present. This name represented the unique covenant relationship between God and His people. It meant that God not only existed, but He was also actively participating in their lives. This designation is considered God's personal name.
Shaddai	Almighty	This definition has two possibilities: mountain, or destroyer. This name represents the awesome, sovereign power of God.

7. Explain why Ruth used "LORD" as she expressed her commitment to Naomi and her people (Ruth 1:17).____

_____

_____

8. Analyze why Naomi used both "LORD" and "Almighty" as she related the events of the past years to the townspeople of Bethlehem (Ruth 1:20–21)._____

_____

_____

_____

9. Why did Boaz use "LORD" when he was speaking to Ruth (Ruth 2:12)? _____

_____

10. In Ruth 4:11−15, "LORD" is used four times. Why would the elders and townspeople make use of this name in this situation? _____

_____

_____

11. What name do you use when addressing God? What pictures of God does this title bring to your mind? _____

_____

_____

_____

12. If you could give yourself a name representing the relationship you've had with God this past year, what would that name be? _____

_____

13. If you were to analyze your present relationship to God, what name would you use for yourself? _____

_____

14. What name do you want to possess as an expression of your relationship to Him a year from now? ten years from now?_____

_____

*15. Prayerfully consult God about how you can begin expressing the characteristics of the name you desire. As you pray, be conscious of how you address Him. What are you communicating by the name or title you use?

5

DECISIONS, DECISIONS

Ruth 1:1–5

"I know it's not the best decision, but it's really the only option that makes any sense. Besides that, it's only temporary, and I have to consider the needs of my family. I'm sure the Lord will understand."

Maybe these were Elimelech's thoughts as he left the Promised Land and moved his family to Moab. To flee from a famine must have seemed very sensible to him. He probably never dreamed that for himself and his sons the sojourn would be for a lifetime.

Elimelech and Naomi were not just moving to a new state with hopes of bringing down the unemployment rate. They were leaving the land God had given to His covenant people. They soon discovered that the security they sought outside of God's provision was only an illusion.

Examining Elimelech's Decision

1. If you had discussed with Elimelech whether he should go to Moab or stay in Bethlehem, what pros and cons would you have considered?

PROS	CONS

2. How long did the family plan to stay in Moab (Ruth 1:1)?_____

   About how long did they stay (Ruth 1:4)?_____

   _____

3. Review God's instructions to His people concerning Moab (Deuteronomy 23:3–6). Why do you think Elimelech disregarded these specific prohibitions?____

_____

_____

4. List the family's original purposes for moving to Moab. Compare this list with the consequences of their move.

Original Purposes for Moving to Moab	Consequences of Moving to Moab

5. What significance did the land hold for the Hebrew people (Genesis 12:1; Deuteronomy 4:1)?_____

_____

_____

6. What statement was Elimelech making to God when he crossed the border into Moab? _____

_____

_____

7. Explain why God had allowed the Promised Land to experience famine during Elimelech's lifetime. (See Leviticus 26:3−5, 14−20.) _____

_____

_____

_____

8. Judges 6:1–6 records the circumstances that some believe coincide with the Book of Ruth. Why does it say these events were happening?_____

_____

_____

Examining Our Own Decisions

9. Identify one of the most difficult decisions you have encountered in the past._____

_____

10. Where did you go for counsel about the decision?_____

_____

_____

11. How did you find relief from the tension and anxiety caused by the decision?_____

_____

_____

12. Would you do anything different if you had a second chance?_____

_____

_____

13. Think of a decision you are facing now and list any Scriptures that give insight into what you should do. (If you feel there are no specific scriptural instructions that address your situation, try this: Search for passages that

give insight into the attitudes you are to exhibit during
the evaluation of this decision.)_____

_____

_____

_____

14. If you find you need to take a specific action or to
    change an attitude in response to the Scriptures you
    have examined, record how you plan to participate in
    the changing process._____

_____

_____

_____

*15. God's people encounter suffering for reasons other than
    making wrong choices. What are these other reasons as
    indicated in the following passages:

    James 1:2–4 _____

_____

_____

    2 Corinthians 1:3–11 _____

_____

_____

    Deuteronomy 8:1–5 _____

_____

_____

6

YOUR GOD SHALL BE MY GOD

Ruth 1:6–18

"Now listen girls, we must be realistic about this. It's ridiculous for you to leave everything and follow me back to Bethlehem. There's no future for you there. You've been so kind to walk this far with me, but I want you both to return to your families now. I can give you nothing. In Moab, at least, you'll have the option to start over again. You've both experienced enough heartache through your association with me; I'll not let you go through any more."

Could this be how Naomi's reasoning with her daughters-in-law would sound today? In their culture it was traditional for foreign brides to return to their own people if a husband died. Therefore the initial reaction of the two younger women is out of the ordinary.

At first they both were determined to accompany Naomi to her homeland. However, as Naomi continued to insist they return to Moab, two different sets of ears were absorbing her arguments. Orpah listened closely to her options for the future. She chose tradition and logic—and we never hear of her again. Ruth refused all options except the one demanded by devotion and faith—and the world has never forgotten her.

Naomi's Logic

1. Explain the major points of Naomi's argument for her daughters-in-law to return to Moab (Ruth 1:8–15).___

_____

_____

_____

_____

2. Why do you think Orpah chose to return to her homeland? What did she gain by reappearing at her Moabite mother's home? What did she lose by saying good-bye to her Israelite mother-in-law?_____

_____

_____

_____

_____

Ruth's Commitment

In the table below, you will find two columns. The left column contains each aspect of Ruth's classic expression of commitment. The right column is to be filled with the actions Ruth took to express her pledge to Naomi. Use the entire Book of Ruth to find the ways Ruth remained true to her promises.

The Promises	The Practical Expressions of Commitment

3. Where you go I will go.

4. Where you stay I will stay.

5. Your people shall be my people.

6. Your God shall be my God.

7. Where you die I will die, and there I will be buried.

8. May nothing but death separate you and me.

Our Personal Commitments

9. What spoken commitments have you made to other people in your life? They may have been the simple but profound words, "I love you." They may have been the words we use too lightly such as, "I'll pray for you." Whatever those words are, see if you can state them in the table below and evaluate the ways you have actively expressed your commitment.

Ideas:

—*If you are married, examine your marriage vows. List each part of those vows in the verbal commitment column and evaluate in the other column your success at expressing those commitments throughout your years of marriage.*

—*You may want to evaluate your commitment to the Lord. What parts of your life have you committed to Him? Do your actions say the same as your words?*

—*Also try evaluating your commitment as a parent, your accountability to your employer, your responsibility to the local church body, your relationship of honor toward your parents, your commitment to your brothers or sisters, or any agreements you have made with a roommate.*

Verbal Commitments	Practical Expressions of Commitment

Verbal Commitments	Practical Expressions of Commitment

10. Maybe you discovered a commitment that you have not maintained consistently. Maybe you cannot continue that commitment; if so, share your withdrawal of commitment so the people involved are not left wondering. If you want to continue the commitment, list it below and choose one action you will take this week to live out your promise._____

_____

_____

_____

11. How many people or causes can we commit ourselves to in the same way Ruth committed herself to Naomi? Explain your answer._____

_____

_____

12. Name the things that cause you to hesitate before you commit yourself to another person._____

_____

_____

_____

*13. What commitment level do you have toward the other members of your Bible study group? How have you expressed your commitment?

7

TRANSFERRED SPIRITUALITY

Ruth 1:19—22; and all the dialogues involving Naomi.

The Book of Ruth takes place in an era of spiritual baton dropping. The generation of Joshua made a sloppy handoff as Israel settled into the Promised Land. During the period of the judges, each generation took its turn around the race track. Lap after lap was run with the same mistakes, the same sins, and the same careless transferal of spiritual truth. Finally in the middle of this frustrating race, one woman quietly but skillfully communicated her faith to the next generation.

The godly commitment of Ruth cannot be observed without considering the woman who helped introduce Yahweh to this Moabite maiden. Something about Naomi and the God she served was irresistible. Ruth must have listened in wonder as she entered a home where feasts and Sabbaths were observed in remembrance of the mighty acts of a personal God. She must have asked Naomi a hundred questions as she learned the proper preparation of foods in accordance with each celebration. Even as the heartaches of death touched them both, Ruth watched Naomi continue to acknowledge Yahweh as the God personally involved in all of life.

Analyzing the Qualities of a Remarkable Woman

We will be looking at four dialogues that demonstrate Naomi's influence on Ruth.

Dialogue #1—Ruth 1:8–15

1. What primary concern did Naomi's words communicate?_____

   _____

2. Through her concern, what attribute was Naomi modeling despite her own poverty and heartache?_____

   _____

Dialogue #2—Ruth 1:20–21

3. How bitter was a widow's life in Old Testament times? (Look up "widow" in a Bible encyclopedia.)_____

   _____

   _____

   _____

4. In Ruth 1:21, Naomi says, "The Lord has afflicted me." What is your reaction to Naomi's words?_____

   _____

   _____

5. What aspects of God's character was Naomi relating to the townswomen in front of Ruth?_____

_____

_____

Dialogue #3—Ruth 2:19–22

6. What attitude did Naomi communicate to Ruth about those who showed kindness to them?_____

_____

_____

7. What part of God's character did Naomi express to Ruth in verse 20?_____

_____

_____

8. Describe the feelings Naomi communicated about Ruth's new job in verse 22._____

_____

_____

Dialogue #4—Ruth 3:1–4

9. Restate in your own words the reason Naomi gives for this detailed planning session._____

_____

_____

10. In this passage, what attribute was Naomi modeling for Ruth?_____

_____

_____

Modeling Spiritual Truth to Others

11. Who has had the most influence on your spiritual development? Explain what that person has done or said to make you hunger for a deeper knowledge of God._____

_____

_____

12. List the people you influence each week. How are you modeling true spirituality to them?_____

_____

_____

_____

13. Choose one person from your list and develop ideas of how you can effectively attract him or her to Christ or how you can help strengthen that person's relationship with God._____

_____

_____

_____

*14. If you have a mother-in-law and/or daughter-in-law, evaluate your relationship with her. What can you do to improve your relationship so that it begins to resemble the commitment between Ruth and Naomi? (If you do not have in-laws, use the same evaluation of mother/daughter or aunt/niece relationships.)

8

A KNIGHT IN SHINING ARMOR

Ruth 2:1–23

> *Now Naomi had a relative on her husband's side, from the clan of Elimelech, a man of standing, whose name was Boaz.*
>
> *—Ruth 2:1*

Until this moment in the story, famine, death, heartache, and poverty had been the focus of the central characters. In the midst of these desperate situations a glimmer of hope is given. Boaz is introduced.

A close look at this announcement soon makes the reader aware that it should have been accompanied by trumpets and banners! Boaz held the possibility of rescuing the two destitute widows because he was related to Naomi.

The phrase "a man of standing" expresses the character of every hero—strong in mind and spirit. Old Testament usage of the phrase usually depicted valor on the battle field, and it is possible that Boaz had been a warrior in those troubled times. However, in the Book of Ruth, it is his wealth, integrity, and influence in the community that gave him a hero's position.

If the book's introduction of Boaz is combined with the meaning of his name, "strength" and "fleetness," the equivalent is Superman!

The graphic picture of chapter 1 is two damsels in distress. Chapter 2 portrays a knight in shining armor galloping toward the women. Here is one who can change the plight of the heroines.

The Lineage of a Hero

Look at the genealogy recorded at the end of the Book of Ruth. The ancestors of Boaz are traced in the Old Testament custom of naming only the men in the family. Turn to Matthew 1:3–6 and read the identical genealogy. Matthew traces the same men but includes three significant women as well. These women, named in the kingly line of Jesus Christ, are all Gentiles. The questions below will help you evaluate the influence two of these foreign women might have had on Boaz.

1. Read Tamar's story in Genesis 38. This story was probably passed down through the generations, and it is likely that Boaz had been told of the episode from which his ancestor Perez had been born. What influence might this story have had on Boaz's response to Ruth and Naomi?_____

_____

_____

2. Read Rahab's story found in Joshua 2:1–24 and 6:24–25. Because of possible exclusions from the genealogies in Ruth and in Matthew, we are uncertain whether

Rahab was Boaz's mother or grandmother. In either case, she would have been well known to Boaz. How might this relationship between Rahab and Boaz have affected Boaz's view of Ruth?_____

_____

_____

A Close Look at Our Hero

3. The entrance of Boaz in our story immediately changes the depressing picture of Ruth and Naomi's poverty. In his first encounter with Ruth, he carefully and sensitively meets her needs. Use the entire chapter to identify Ruth's needs and Boaz's creative provisions. Record your findings in the table below:

Ruth's Needs	Boaz's Provisions
Physical:	
Emotional:	

Ruth's Needs	Boaz's Provisions
Spiritual:	

4. What did the law require Boaz to do for the poor and for the foreigners who came to glean in his fields (Leviticus 19:9–10; 23:22)?_____

_____

_____

5. How would you evaluate Boaz's obedience to this requirement of the law?_____

_____

_____

6. List all the things Boaz did that were not required by the letter of the law._____

_____

_____

_____

7. What does Boaz's level of obedience demonstrate about his character?_____

_____

_____

A Close Look at Ourselves

8. Read James 2:1–13. What is the requirement for relating to the poor today?_____

_____

_____

*9. Prayerfully evaluate how your personal actions and attitudes measure up to these instructions._____

_____

_____

10. The *letter* of these instructions is: Do not show favoritism. Write what you think the *spirit* of the commands is (James 2:8)._____

_____

_____

_____

11. Describe a situation in which you observed someone else expressing the spirit of this command to the poor.___

_____

_____

_____

12. How can you go beyond lack of favoritism to loving the needy as yourself this week? Review your table on pages 55–56 for some creative ideas from Boaz._____

_____

_____

_____

9

INITIATORS BEFORE A SOVEREIGN GOD

Ruth 3:1–18

Ruth's response to Naomi's well-designed plan expressed total, unquestioning obedience. Somehow it couldn't have been quite that easy. Ruth must have had uncontrollable butterflies as she left Naomi that night and made her way toward the most important moment of her life.

How would you have felt? Try to imagine yourself crouching in the shadows, waiting for the harvesters to finish their threshing. At each close sound you would probably jump inside and reappraise the security of your hiding place. Your eyes would ache to find the campfire of Boaz. Making a mistake about his location would ruin everything. Once you spot him, your eyes lock on his position among the wheat. You begin memorizing the best pathway to reach him. Finally your peripheral vision reveals dying campfires as weary threshers fall asleep one by one.

As the hillside becomes quiet, you are certain your

heartbeat can be heard by everyone. Here you are in a strange land, counting on an unorthodox plan to save your own future and the future of your beloved mother-in-law.

The peaceful repose of the threshers sharply contrasts your tense alertness. This stillness is your signal to begin your delicate mission. What if Boaz is displeased by the way you approach him? What if he sends you away in disgust? You have enjoyed a short time of acceptance and respect in this foreign land, but after tonight it might be destroyed. How will Boaz respond when he is awakened on this night? The next few hours will determine the direction of the rest of your life. It has to work. The whole idea seems ridiculous in this quiet moment, and you feel like running all the way back to Moab—but it's too late.

The time to make your move is now. Although your hiding place seemed precarious during the waiting hours, now it seems like a haven compared to the threshing floor that you must inch across toward the sleeping man. You're sure he will hear your footsteps and be enraged that you dare come to this place. Maybe he will even question your motives and all the kind encouragement from this godly man will be over.

Finally you reach him and lie tensely at his feet. Surely the loud pounding of your heart will awaken him and everyone else. Sleep is impossible on a night like tonight.

Suddenly he starts and every muscle in your body stands ready for flight. Before you can utter a word, he demands to know who you are. In the blackness of the night you cannot see the paternal eyes that once expressed concern for you. It's impossible to make out the mouth that formed words of comfort during many of your most difficult days in Bethlehem. All the speeches you rehearsed from your hiding place vanish from your mind. All you can blurt out is your name and your need.

The demanding voice that pierced the silence suddenly

changes to a soothing, peaceful whisper. The voice speaks blessings on you and reassures you of respect. His words, "Don't be afraid," cause you to relax. He knew from your answer that you were terrified. The words of reassurance continue as Boaz expresses his desire to see you cared for. He promises in his careful way that he will take charge of all the details.

All your apprehensions disappear as he explains his plan of action. He quietly but firmly vows to take up your case. He can be trusted, and you sink back to the floor totally exhausted and totally relieved. Your part is over, and you can rest now.

The next thing you know, Boaz is gently trying to awaken you. It's obvious that the part of the night you slept, he didn't. He seems excited and determined. Will he soon be your husband? You have no time to contemplate the future, for he is instructing you to hurry home before you are recognized. It's his turn for trembling hands as he eagerly fills your shawl with an abundant gift for Naomi.

Initiating a Solution to Ruth's Need

All three of the main characters were busy in this chapter. Each one participated in solving the dilemma faced by Ruth and Naomi.

1. Naomi's first words in chapter 3 could also be expressed, "I feel responsible to see you settled in life. I want you to be well cared for." What factors from the story made it the right time for Naomi to pursue a better life for Ruth?_____
   _____
   _____

2. What do Ruth's words in verse 5 reveal about her appraisal of Naomi? What kind of a person could you say those words to?_____ __

_____

_____

3. How does she introduce herself in verse 9? What is she expressing by the identification she chose to use?_____

_____

_____

4. What is the meaning of her request, "Spread the corner of your garment over me?" (You may want to check a commentary or look at Ezekiel 16:8 where the same phrase is used.)_____

_____

_____

_____

5. What is she communicating in the last phrase of her petition, "since you are a kinsman-redeemer"?_____

_____

_____

_____

6. Boaz's response in 3:10—11 gives us a wealth of information about Ruth. Make a list of these insights:

Verse 10a—

Verse 10b—

Verse 11—

7. In this narrative, the vow that usually receives all the attention is Ruth's commitment to Naomi in chapter 1. However, in Ruth 3:13 another vow is made that deserves equal attention. What impact would this reply have made on Ruth?_____ _____

_____

_____

_____

8. At the close of the threshing floor scene, Boaz performs two acts on Ruth's behalf. Record those acts and describe their significance to Ruth._____

_____

_____

_____

9. What does Naomi tell Ruth to do next (verse 18)? How do you feel when this is the only thing left to do?_____

_____

_____

_____

10. Each of these main characters has expressed his or her devotion to a sovereign God in the previous chapters. By word or deed they have also demonstrated belief in His interventions and His involvement in each of their lives. However, in chapter 3 they all seem to take matters into their own hands—or do they? The table on the next page contains four references that record the contributions made toward solving the widows' dilemma. Fill in the chart by identifying the characters and their contributions.

Character	Contribution	Reference
		3:1–4
		3:5,9,14–15
		3:10–13,15; 4:1
		3:18

Initiating Solutions to Our Needs

11. When should you initiate solutions to the needs you encounter, and when should you stand by and let God do something without your intervention?_____

_____

_____

_____

12. If you decide to initiate action, are you opposing belief in a sovereign God? Explain._____

_____

_____

_____

*13. Identify a difficulty you are presently facing. On the chart on the next page, put your name by the stage of the solution process you are in. Write out how you will participate in this stage.

Name	Solution Stages	How I will participate
	creative planning	
	complete obedience	
	committed action	
	confident waiting	

10

A DAY IN COURT

Ruth 4:1–10

I thought the siren sounded close. When I checked, there were the flashing red lights in *my* rear view mirror. As I pulled to the side of the road and stopped, I frantically tried to figure out what I had done to deserve such undivided attention.

The police officer approached the car and chatted about the busload of children I had just passed illegally. Sure enough, on the opposite side of a five-lane highway was a school bus unloading its precious cargo of little children. I had zoomed past without stopping and was awarded a one hundred and sixty dollar ticket. I was thrilled to know the state cared so much for the protection of its children, but the fine did seem to be a bit much.

The officer encouraged me to appeal for a reduced fine in traffic court, and I readily took his advice. I returned home and filled out the appropriate papers. I certainly wished the matter could be settled that day (preferably before my husband returned from work).

Finally, correspondence from the county came in the mail. My day in court would be eighteen months from the date of the infraction. Eighteen months to await a decision.

How convenient it would have been to live during the societal simplicity that permitted Boaz to settle a legal matter the very next day. As he made his way that morning to the city gates, he was heading for the center of community affairs. The gates were primarily a place to settle legal matters, but they were also the location for any major gathering. A few short hours after Ruth's request, Boaz had assembled all the people needed to settle the matter of Naomi's land and Ruth's marriage.

The Background of Redemption

The word "redemption" may bring several pictures to the twentieth-century mind. However, most modern images of redemption are far different from the legal transaction represented by this word in Hebrew culture. Let's explore the background of this concept in order to better understand Boaz's "day in court."

1. What instructions had God given His people concerning the redemption of land (Leviticus 25: 23–25)?_____

_____

_____

2. How were these instructions obeyed in the Book of Ruth?_____

_____

_____

3. Read Leviticus 25:47–55 carefully. What instructions had God given concerning the redemption of people?

_____

_____

_____

4. After Boaz approaches the nearest relative with Naomi's forced land sale, he brings up another issue. What did God require of the widow's family (Deuteronomy 25:5–6)?_____

_____

_____

5. Neither Boaz nor the close relative was Elimelech's brother. (Boaz's reference to "our brother" in verse 3 means a larger circle of relatives.) Because they were not brothers in the same household, the letter of the law did not require them to marry Elimelech's widow or his son's widow. What appeal does Boaz use for Ruth's marriage (Deuteronomy 25:6b; Ruth 4:5)?_____

_____

_____

6. From Ruth 4:4 to 4:6 the closest relative has a change of heart. Why do you think he relinquished his rights to Boaz?_____

_____

_____

The Qualifications of a Redeemer

The Hebrew word used for redeemer in Ruth is *goel*. The best translation of the word is "kinsman-redeemer."

As we have already discovered, a kinsman-redeemer could move into civil court and recover property or people. Therefore he was capable of delivering land and people from the penalty of the law. If a portion of land had been sold, he had the right to buy it back. If a person had sold himself into servitude because of poverty, the redeemer had the right to buy the person's freedom. However, in order to qualify as a kinsman-redeemer certain prerequisites had to be fulfilled.

The basic qualifications of a kinsman-redeemer are listed below. Use the list to evaluate the two men who were considering the redemption transaction on behalf of Naomi and Ruth.

7. If the closer relative is held up beside the qualifications of a redeemer, where does he fall short?

Qualifications	The Unnamed Relative
a. He must be a close relative.	a.
b. He must perform the redemption willingly.	b.
c. He must possess the price of redemption.	c.
d. He must be free himself.	d.

8. How does Boaz compare to the same list?

Qualifications	Boaz
a. He must be a close relative.	a.
b. He must perform the redemption willingly.	b.
c. He must possess the price of redemption.	c.
d. He must be free himself.	d.

Is Christ Qualified to Be Our Redeemer?

Redemption in the Book of Ruth cannot be studied without drawing parallels with personal redemption through Jesus Christ. Before the perfect, Holy God all are found desperately lacking. Man's only hope for a relationship with God and a release from eternal death is through the intervention of a kinsman-redeemer. Jesus Christ has willingly paid the price for freedom from spiritual death through the costly sacrifice of His own life. He has not only purchased this freedom, but He has also welcomed those who believe in Him into an intimate relationship with Himself for all eternity. As Boaz was to Ruth on a physical level, Christ is to us on a spiritual level. Both the Old Testament and the New Testament claim that He is the Redeemer of the human race. Let's put those claims to the test.

9. Evaluate Jesus Christ the same way the close relative and Boaz were evaluated. Is Jesus really qualified to be our Redeemer? Use a concordance to find Scriptures supporting Christ's ability to redeem. Look first at the New Testament entries under the following words: "redeem," "redeemed," "redeemer," and "redemption."

Qualifications	Jesus Christ
a. He must be a close relative.	a.
b. He must perform the redemption willingly.	b.

Qualifications	Jesus Christ

c. He must possess the price   c.
of redemption.

d. He must be free himself.   d.

10. What difference does it make to know that Jesus Christ is qualified to provide for your redemption and eternal life?_____

_____

_____

*11. Use the last moments of your study time to review the chart of Christ's qualifications as a Redeemer. Tell your Kinsman-Redeemer how you personally feel about the costly price He willingly paid for your spiritual life and freedom.

11

A TIME TO RESPOND

Ruth 4:11—17

In our hurried age, there seems to be a time for everything but reflecting. We rush to the next event without taking time to evaluate or enjoy the experiences of the day before. Perhaps some of us are losing the art of celebration and praise. Maybe through this chapter we can restore the ability of responding to our God and reinstate it as a priority.

The climax of the story of Ruth is over. The qualified redeemer has legally completed the transaction needed to provide for Ruth and Naomi, but the story continues. The townspeople respond to the transaction, and Ruth responds to her redeemer-husband. The townswomen respond to God's blessing through the child Obed, and Naomi responds to the removal of her sorrow.

We all held our breath through the first part of chapter 4 when the hero of the story looked as though he might lose the heroine. Now the conflict is resolved. Boaz is the redeemer of the widows and their land. It is not the time to rush to the next problem; it is time to celebrate! It is not the time to merely go on with life, it is time to pause and acknowledge the One who has resolved the ache of emptiness. It is the time to respond to the God whose loyal love is always active toward His people. It is the time to praise, to bless, and to celebrate!

A Time to Bless

1. As the townspeople respond to the redemption, they ask the Lord to make Ruth like Rachel and Leah. Why do you think they chose these women?_____

   _____

   _____

2. The townspeople also ask a blessing for Boaz. To understand the significance of their words, remember that the Levirate marriage was a sacrificial act of concern. How might Boaz have felt when the townspeople spoke the words found in Ruth 4:11?_____

   _____

   _____

A Time to Respond

All through the narrative, Ruth has been responding to Boaz's kindnesses. The following questions parallel this woman's responses to her kinsman-redeemer with your responses to your Kinsman-Redeemer.

3. In Ruth 2:10, what did Ruth's actions and words express about her character?_____

   _____

Bowing is not customary in Western culture. What would it mean to you if you observed someone bowing with his or her face to the ground in response to God's undeserved kindness? Do you feel comfortable in this prayer posture?_____

_____

_____

4. How does Ruth respond in 2:13?_____

_____

_____

What expressions of comfort and kindness has God directed toward you recently? Have you taken the time to acknowledge these before Him with thanksgiving?__

_____

_____

5. In Ruth 2:14, Ruth doesn't greet Boaz's offer for food with a polite, "No thank you; I'm just fine." What is she expressing by receiving his provisions?_____

_____

_____

How self-sufficient are you? Do you go it alone in your spiritual life, or do you agree with God's appraisal of your need by receiving His provisions, i.e., wisdom from His Word, comfort through the Spirit, strength through prayer?

_____

_____

6. In Ruth 3:9, we find our humble responder doing some bold initiating. Why was this action appropriate?_____

_____

_____

We are needy before God, and He has invited us to come to Him with our cares. How often do you exercise this privilege as God's child?_____

7. What is Ruth expressing by her response to Boaz in 3:13–14a?_____

_____

_____

When you come to understand instructions through God's Word, how complete is your obedience? How complete is your trust in God?_____

_____

A Time to Celebrate

Ruth 4:13–17 allows us to peek in on a very meaningful baby shower. Naomi is affectionately cradling her grandson, and the townswomen are present to help her celebrate.

8. The townswomen attending the shower did something unusual; they named the child (verse 17). What is the meaning of the name they gave? What significance does the name have for Obed's position in this family?_

_____

_____

9. As the townswomen speak in verses 14–15, their words reflect the components of true celebration. Can you identify the three components?

a. Verse 14a—

b. Verses 14b–15a—

c. Verse 15b—

10. Are these components evident in the events you celebrate in your family, in your church, or among your friends? Which ones are included? Which ones are missing?_____

_____

_____

11. Building traditions around remembering God's faithfulness to your family builds strong relationships between those who have shared the occasion. How can you incorporate these celebration components in your next family holiday?_____

_____

_____

12

WILL I ALWAYS FEEL THIS EMPTINESS?

Ruth 4:18–21

We all experience birth and death. We pass so quickly from growing up to growing old. Despite the uncompromising adherence to health food and the consistent use of beauty secrets, another generation will eventually take our place. Our brief appearance in history will be over. To know that God is working out His sovereign, eternal purposes brings comfort during this rapid passage of years. As we experience the joys and sorrows of each life stage, we are being molded into people who have a greater capacity to know God. What a comfort to know that the same God who carried Ruth and Naomi through their seasons of emptiness and fullness is the same God who is personally guiding our lives.

The Cycles of Emptiness and Fullness

The Book of Ruth is a story with a pastoral setting. The changing condition of the land reflects changes for the main characters. For example, as the land experienced famine, Naomi and Ruth experienced loss. As the land produced a fruitful harvest, Ruth conceived a long-awaited child. It is as if the progression of the story line is echoed in the condition of the land.

1. Using the following table, compare the the land's condition with the story line. Beside each reference describe the plight of the land and the plight of the characters at that point in the story.

Reference	Condition of the Land	Condition of the People
1:1−5		
1:6−22		
2:1−23		

Reference	Condition of the Land	Condition of the People
3:1–4:21		

2. Throughout the story, both the land and the characters experience a cycle from emptiness to fullness. This second table helps you trace this theme through the narrative.

Emptiness	Fullness
Record the destitute circumstances found in the following verses: 1:1–4	List the *references* and *incidents* that resolve the former times of emptiness:

Emptiness	Fullness
1:11−13	
1:20−21	

The Unchanging God

As the land and the people experienced emptiness and fullness, God was working out His sovereign purposes. His work involved not only the individual lives of two widows but also the entire nation of Israelites.

3. In Ruth 1:13 and 1:20−21, Naomi describes her life's most difficult season. Even at her deepest moments of loss, what did she possess?_____

_____

4. Compare Naomi's seasons of fullness with her season of emptiness. How many years did she know emptiness? What parts of her life were years of fullness?___

_____

_____

_____

_____

5. Naomi and Boaz testify to the same aspect of God's character in Ruth 1:8 and 2:12. How can this part of God's character be a comfort in times of trial?_____

_____

_____

6. Compare the first time the LORD is mentioned in the Book of Ruth (1:6) with the last time (4:14). What aspect of God's character does He demonstrate through these actions on behalf of His nation and of one individual?_____

_____

_____

_____

7. After the Lord had restored Naomi's family through Obed, what message for the nation is contained in the genealogy (Ruth 4:18–21)?_____

_____

_____

8. With what man does the genealogy conclude? What was the spiritual tenor of his life (Acts 13:22)? What was his contribution to the nation of Israel (2 Samuel 3:17–18)?_____

_____

_____

9. This same genealogy appears in the New Testament (Matthew 1:3–6). What man is the focus of this genealogy? Describe his life's significance._____

_____

_____

The Seasons of Our Lives

Chart below the seasons of your life. In the left column, record your life in relation to the emptiness/fullness theme seen in Ruth. In the right-hand column, list the ways God has worked out His purposes through these seasons. So many times in the midst of a season of emptiness we see nothing of His purposes; we only hurt. Maybe this chart will help to bring insight to the difficult seasons you have experienced.

Date	Seasons I have Experienced	God's Sovereign Work

Date	Seasons I have Experienced	God's Sovereign Work

*10. Use the last moments of your study time to thank God for the ways He worked through the empty and full times in Ruth's and Naomi's lives. Use the chart above to thank Him for His work in your personal life. Then identify the present season you are experiencing and renew your trust in His sovereign control.

As you remain faithful to Him during each season of life, may you be richly rewarded by Yahweh, the God of Israel, under whose wings you have learned to take daily refuge.

BIBLIOGRAPHY

Barber, Cyril J. *Ruth: An Expositional Commentary.* Chicago: Moody Press, 1983.

Cundall, Arthur E. and Leon Morris. *Judges and Ruth: Tyndale Old Testament Commentaries,* ed. D.J. Wiseman. Downers Grove: InterVarsity Press, 1968.

Enns, Paul P. *Ruth: Bible Study Commentary.* Grand Rapids: Zondervan, 1982.

Lewis, Arthur H. *Judges, Ruth: Everyman's Bible Commentary.* Chicago: Moody Press, 1979.

McQuilkin, J. Robertson. *Understanding and Applying the Bible.* Chicago: Moody Press, 1983.

Rauber, D.F. "The Book of Ruth" in *Literary Interpretations of Biblical Narratives,* ed. Kenneth R. Gros Louis with James S. Ackerman and Thayer S. Warshaw. Nashville: Abingdon Press, 1974.

Ryken, Leland. *The Literature of the Bible.* Grand Rapids: Zondervan, 1974.

Tenney, Merrill C., ed. *The Zondervan Pictorial Encyclopedia of the Bible.* Grand Rapids: Zondervan, 1975, 1976.